ASSIGNMENT JONESVILLE

ASSIGNMENT JONESVILLE

A News Reporting Workbook

Revised Edition

NICHOLAS N. PLASTERER

Louisiana State University Press, Baton Rouge

ISBN 0-8071-0037-4
Copyright © 1966, 1971 by
Louisiana State University Press
Manufactured in the United States of America
1977 printing

PREFACE

This workbook has two goals in training the student
reporter. First, it will give him practical experience in the actual writing of news stories. Second,
it should help him to develop such attributes of a
good reporter as judgment, responsibility, alertness
and resourcefulness.

The workbook is divided into three parts. The first
two contain fact situations, while the third part is
devoted to reference materials.

Many reporting students at first have difficulty with
leads. Accordingly, Part I contains 15 fact situations suitable for writing leads. The fact situations
are brief, but even so the student must be selective.
Otherwise, he will be unable to hold his leads to the
usual 30- or 35-word maximum.

Part II has fact situations for 75 complete news
stories. Parts I and II should provide the instructor
with enough material for a two-semester course. He
may even have some choice of assignments. The fact
situations in the second half of Part II are generally
somewhat longer and/or complicated than those in the
first half.

For the convenience of the student the assignment sheets
have been perforated. Thus he may detach the pages
before turning to the reference section for checking
names and facts. This section includes a scale-model
city directory, city, county and area maps, and a brief
morgue or library.

As much responsibility as possible is placed upon the
student. For each assignment he must consult the city
directory for middle initials, addresses, correct
spelling of names and perhaps for identification. (The
directory is only representative; not all names

appearing in fact situations are listed in it.) There
also may be instances of incorrect spelling of words
other than names. The student is advised to have a
dictionary handy when working on an assignment.

Also, the fact situation may not necessarily be complete in itself. Additional information for some of
the assignments will be found in the morgue or library
section. The student will not be so advised when an
assignment is made. It will be his responsibility to
check both the city directory and the morgue portion of
this workbook. He may or may not find additional pertinent information for the assignment in question.

The fact situations will not follow any particular
style. Actually, a policy of inconsistency will be
detected. It will be up to the student to make his
story conform to the style book prescribed for the
course.

A good reporter makes it a point to learn the city of
publication and the circulation area. Accordingly, the
student reporter is expected to familiarize himself with
all reference materials in this workbook.

Obviously, the city directory and the morgue section are
incomplete, compared with those used by a daily newspaper
in a medium-sized city. They are intended to be merely
representative. However, they will provide the student
with practical problems in the use of such reference
materials. The names of most of the persons living
within the city limits of Jonesville who are involved
in the fact situations will be found in the city
directory. Also, in an appreciable number of the assignments the morgue section must be used before a
satisfactory news story can be written. Furthermore,
locations and directions in the fact situations should
be verified by using the city, county and circulation-
area maps.

The usual newspaper morgue is comprised largely of
clippings of previous stories about individuals, organizations, institutions and business firms. Other reference materials, such as annual reports and brochures,
also are filed. For the sake of brevity, the morgue
section of this workbook is primarily in the form of

summarized facts, with occasional excerpts from ficti-
tious news stories.

Two reference-material tests are included in the workbook. If the reporting course is presented in two
semesters, it is suggested that one test be given at
the beginning of each semester. The student will be
required to familiarize himself with the reference
materials in order to find the answers to the test
questions.

The newspaper reporter seldom writes his stories from
source material comprised of structurally perfect
sentences. Instead, he generally is using notes taken
during a personal or telephone interview or while
covering a meeting, or from a release or memo obviously written by a nonprofessional. Accordingly, the
fact situations in this workbook will be given in
summary or note form wherever possible or feasible.
This will necessitate original writing on the part of
the student.

An exception in presentation of the fact situation, of
course, will be coverage of a speech when the text is
included. In such case the problem will be one of condensing the material to a story of appropriate length.
The student must summarize the information. Most of
the story will be in the form of indirect quotations.
The instructor will give specific, additional instruc-
tions for each speech assignment. It is suggested that
a limit be placed upon the amount of direct quotation--
perhaps two to four column-inches. This will force the
student to paraphrase for most of the story, thereby
giving him valuable experience in condensing and com-
bining material of a speech text.

Our mythical city of Jonesville, county seat of Adams
County, is in the population range of 40,000 to 50,000.
Black Creek, normally a small stream, cuts through the
northern edge of the city. Grossboro, the state capital,
lies 75 miles to the west. Jonesville has two daily
newspapers, both owned by one company and operated from
the same plant. Some of the stories will be written for
the Sun, a morning paper, and the rest for the Star, an
evening paper.

All stories must be typewritten, double spaced, with an
inch margin on each side. For most assignments the instructor should perhaps prescribe a length limitation.
This may be in the form of a general approximation--
a minimum length or a minimum-maximum range--with the
limits in column-inches. A column-inch may be computed
at four typewritten lines of about 65 typewriter
characters each.

The student is instructed to copyread all stories
carefully before submitting them. Orthodox copy-
reading symbols are to be used.

CONTENTS

PART III

City Directory and Newspaper
Morgue or Library

PART I

LEAD ASSIGNMENTS

1 / CYCLE TRIP

You're a reporter for the Sun. It's a Tuesday late in
April. The city editor tells you to take phone call from
Bruce D. MacDonald. MacDonald tells you he's president
of the Grace Methodist Men's Club. He says club is spon-
soring a bicycle trip this Saturday--for boys and girls
of church, ages 10 to 14. Leave Saturday morning at 9
on State Road 9 at city limits. Go on State Road 9 one
mile, then two miles on Himes Road to Stone Creek.
Steak roast at noon. Games. Return Saturday afternoon.

2 / GARDEN CLUB

You're a reporter for the Star. It's early February.
Mrs. Philip E. O'Brien has phoned Star and you talk to
her. She is president of Central Garden Club. She says
club will open 24th season Feb. 17. Meeting to be at
O'Brien home. Group to discuss raising spring flowers.
Meeting to start at 9:30 a.m.

3 / DOGS

Post Office is on your beat. Postmaster Howard L. Eckart
asks you to write a story for him. He says several mail
carriers in past few weeks have been bitten by dogs. He
wants you to write story--ask residents to cooperate, keep
dogs tied or fenced. He says remind people city ordinance
prohibits letting dogs run loose.

3

4 / BOOK

You're a Sun reporter and Dexter University is on your
beat. It's February. You are told to talk to Dr.
Clinton H. Greene. He tells you he recently finished
writing a college textbook, "Geography of the Western
States." He says word has come from Universal Publish-
ing Co. of Chicago. Universal will publish his book.
It will be on the market before next fall's classes.

5 / ENGINEERING

Dr. Vernon M. Randall, dean of Dexter's College of
Engineering, says Dexter's 7th annual Mechanical Engineering short course will be held Friday, Saturday and
Sunday, March 15, 16 and 17. It's for professional
engineers from throughout the state. New techniques
will be presented.

6 / SALADS

Miss Rose Martin, professor of home economics at Dexter,
tells you she will be at annual convention of the State
Restaurant Association at Grossboro. Convention to be
held Friday and Saturday, March 22 and 23. Miss Martin
will demonstrate how to prepare appetizing salads.

7 / RESIGNS

You're city hall reporter for Star. It's middle of
November. Mayor Alvin C. Baker says he has a story for
you. Joseph E. Underwood has been assistant city manager
for four years. However, he has resigned as of Dec. 31.
He's been appointed city manager of Oxford. Will take
over new job Jan. 1.

8 / GARBAGE

City Manager Arthur E. Bailey tells you that a change
will have to be made in garbage collection. Garbage now
picked up three times a week. But the change--to be
picked up only twice a week; shortage of help and increased
costs make it necessary. This new schedule will start
next week.

9 / POOL

It's the middle of April. City Manager Bailey says he
has workmen making repairs to the pool in City Park.
The repairs should be all wound up before May 1. That's
the date Bailey has scheduled for the opening of the
pool.

10 / HOLDUP

You're police reporter for Star. You get details of a
holdup from Detective William R. Spencer, who is investi-
gating it. He says a man went into the Jonesville Cafe
about 8 last night and held it up. Henry B. Aikens, proprietor of cafe, said man was armed with revolver. He
described him: blonde, about 25 years old, about 6 feet
tall, weighed about 170. Ordered Aikens to give him
money from cash register. Man got about $180.

11 / WINDSHIELD

Patrolman Fred C. Dennam of City Police says a car was
damaged last night; lucky not a serious accident. Peter
S. Glaviano, 3819 N. Clay St., driving home about 8:30
when windshield was smashed. Rock thrown. Glaviano saw
two small boys run after rock hit windshield. Said he
almost lost control of car, almost hit another car coming
from other direction.

12 / SNATCHERS

Police Chief Alvin E. Jackson says because of several purse
snatchings in past week he would like to advise women shop-
pers. Most of the purse snatchings have been done by boys
10 or 12 years old; grab purse and run, usually down an
alley. In most cases the women have been holding purses
loosely. He said get a better grip on your purse. In
several cases, woman had a firm grip and the boy gave
up and ran away empty handed.

13 / ALUMNI

You're a reporter for the Sun. It's September. Rev.
Joseph R. Dickerson, pastor of First Presbyterian Church,
says he feels proud. He's an alumnus of Calhoun College at
Walton. Says he's been invited to speak there Saturday,
Oct. 20; for alumni luncheon at annual Homecoming.
Dickerson graduated from Calhoun in 1951, then attended
theological seminary.

14 / LEAVES

It's October. You are a reporter for the Star. You check
Fire Station. Chief William N. Kennedy says things quiet
except for shed that burned to ground yesterday about 5:30
p.m. John M. Weyerhauser, 3816 Oxford St., was burning
leaves; fire got out of control and set tool shed on fire.
Shed and contents destroyed; about $800 damage, Kennedy
says.

15 / DISPLAY

It's a Monday in April. You're the Star schools reporter.
Miss Linda A. Norwood, principal of Lampton Elementary
School, says fourth annual art display at the school
Thursday from 7 to 8:30 p.m. Art work done by school
pupils of Lampton Elementary will be shown. Parents of
children of the school invited. Coffee, soft drinks
and cookies will be served.

PART II

STORY ASSIGNMENTS

1 / LEHMANN HONORED

Dinner meeting tonight in Fulton Hotel, sponsored
jointly by the Jonesville Engineering Society and
Dexter University College of Engineering. You are
a reporter for the Sun, covering the meeting for
tomorrow morning's paper.

Presiding: Clinton E. Pearson, president of Jonesville
Engineering Society. Present: Members of society,
faculty members of College of Engineering, several
guests. Total present: About 150. Music: Central
High School Choir; Glenn D. Stephens, director.
Purpose of meeting: To honor Harold L. Lehmann.
Native of Jonesville. Now living in state capital,
Grossboro. Retires 15th of next month; to move back
to Jonesville soon.

You learn this information about Mr. Lehmann in talks
given during the meeting and through interviews after
the meeting: Graduate, Central High School, Jonesville,
1930; graduate, Dexter university, B.S. degree in
engineering, 1930. Took job in 1934 with Richardson
Construction company. Lehmann one of founders and first
president of Jonesville Engineering Society. Left
Richardson company in 1941 to take job with State Highway
Department. Promoted to chemical testing engineer in
1950; in 1958 promoted to director of research, his
present job. Supervises work of 40 specialists in
research and testing of all materials used by the
department in road and bridge construction.

A pioneer in the field of testing and research of highway
materials, nationally recognized authority. Has given
more than a dozen technical papers at national and international forums. Is a member of Advisory Committee on
Asphalt Research of American Association of State Highway
Officials.

After dinner, music by choir. Then Pearson calls on

11

several who praise Lehmann. Roy B. Richards of Grossboro,
state director of highways, tells of some of the things
Lehmann has accomplished while with Highway Department.
"Because of his long service to the people of the state
the honor extended to Mr. Lehmann tonight is well deserved,"
Richards says.

Others speak briefly: John T. O'Neill of Lafayette,
president of State Engineering Society; Alvin C. Baker,
mayor of Jonesville.

Then plaque is given; recognizes Lehmann's long service
and accomplishments in highway materials testing and
research with Highway Department. Dr. Vernon M. Randle,
dean, College of Engineering, presents plaque; says Mr.
Lehmann is "one of the most illustrious graduates" of
the College of Engineering.

2 / JACKSON LEAVING

You are a Sun reporter. It is early in April. Dexter
University is on your beat and you are making your
rounds on the campus. You ask to see the president,
Dr. Gardiner. Dr. Gardiner tells you he has an
important story.

Dr. Gardiner says that Dr. Jackson, dean of the College
of Arts and Sciences, resigned today; effective June 10.
Dr. Jackson to be the new president of Calhoun College,
Walton. Calhoun is supported by the Presbyterian church.
You recall that a couple of months ago the Sun carried
story that the present president was retiring some time
this year.

Dr. Gardiner says Jackson joined Dexter faculty in 1958
as an assistant professor of history; dean of College of
Arts and Sciences since 1970.

"Dr. Jackson has performed a great service at Dexter,
first as a member of the faculty, then as dean of the
College of Arts and Sciences," said Dr. Gardiner. "His
leaving will be felt deeply by Dexter personnel and
students. However, we cannot stand in the way of his
advancement to the presidency of Calhoun College. I am
certain that he will prove to be an illustrous president
for that excellent institution."

After you leave Dr. Gardiner, you go to interview Jackson.
Jackson says his position as president of Calhoun is
effective July 1. In answer to your questions, he gives
you other information.

Jackson a native of Detroit; born 1930; B.A. degree,
Hillsdale College, 1952; member of Phi Beta Kappa,
honorary scholastic fraternity. M.A., Ph.D., University
of Michigan. Taught at Olivet College two years before
coming to Dexter. Member of American Association of
University Professors.

13

Lives with wife and two children at 500 W. Zinnia av.
Member of First Presbyterian Church of Jonesville; also
member of its board of deacons. Member of local Exchange
Club, president of club, 1964. Active, annual campaigns
of United Fund for several years; chairman of professional
division last year. Member of Prairie Lodge No. 127,F.&A.M.
Author of 2 history textbooks, one on South America, other
on Central America.

Jackson says he and his family will move to Walton about
June 15.

You return to office. From morgue you get clipping of
story announcing resignation of current president of
Calhoun College; appeared in Sun in January of this
year. His name is Dr. George W. Carpenter. Submitted
resignation to board of trustees in January of this
year. Board accepted resignation, effective June 30.
Dr. Carpenter, faculty member of Calhoun for 9 years;
then dean of men 7 years; president of Calhoun for past
18 years. He and Mrs. Carpenter will remain in Walton
for the summer; move to Florida in September.

Write story for tomorrow's Sun.

It's the middle of May; you are attending a dinner tonight
in Fulton Hotel. Meeting sponsored by College of Arts
and Sciences of Dexter University. You are covering
meeting for tomorrow morning's Sun.

Dr. Howard H. Jackson, dean of College of Arts and
Sciences, presides. Dinner is honoring Dr. Philip
Spence; professor and chairman of History department;
retiring June 10. Brief talks given by Dr. Gardiner,
president of Dexter; Alvin E. Baker, mayor; Frederick
T. Jarrold of Bradley, president of Student Council.
They pay tribute to Spence. About 150 people present.
Music by Dexter Choir; under direction of Prof. Clarence
H. Reid.

You learn this about Spence in talks during the meeting
and interviews afterwards: Graduate, Erie High School,
1929. Graduated, Grossboro College, 1933, B.A. degree.
M.A. degree, University of Chicago, 1935. History
instructor, Bradley U., 1935-37. Graduate student, U.
of Chicago, 1937-39; Ph.D. degree, 1939. Assistant
professor, Dexter U., 1939-45; associate prof., 1945-52;
promoted to professor, 1952. Named chairman of History
Department, 1963. Author of two books, History of
Northwestern United States and Challenge of the
Continental Divide. Also author of about 20 short
stories on northwest.

More information: Member of Phi Beta Kappa; Grace
Methodist church; Kiwanis club. Active in United Fund
campaigns. Two sons, James B. Spence, lawyer, Grossboro;
Francis W., instructor, Purdue University.

At the dinner Dr. Gardiner praises him as one of Dexter's
most outstanding professors. Jackson announces members
of Dexter faculty have bought Spence a set of Encyclopaedia
Brittannica. Jarrold says Spence one of most popular
professors on campus. Mayor Baker says Jonesville

fortunate to have Dexter university; Spence one of most respected faculty members.

Spencer tells you he and wife will continue to live in Jonesville; will spend most of this summer in the Northwest; Spencer doing some historical research. Also will make trip to Alaska. Back to Jonesville in the fall; will finish a novel he's writing on the northwest; also will write some short stories.

Gardiner says successor to Spencer as chairman of department will be announced June 1.

4 / GROCERY CONVENTION

You are a reporter for the Star, Jonesville's afternoon
newspaper. The State Retail Food Dealers association
holding convention in Fulton Hotel. You are assigned
to cover it.

Convention opened yesterday afternoon. Registration
at 3 p.m. First business session at 4; reports made by
committees. Fred T. Wilson of Angola, president of
association, presides at all sessions.

Dinner meeting yesterday evening. Homer R. Williams,
Louisville, Kentucky, president of National Association
of Retail Grocers is speaker. Statements include: Last
year, 63 million family units in United States, 1.5
million more than year before; within 10 years, 85 million
units. Also, 6 billion more pounds of food sold last year
than year before. Also, change in trend; housewives
using more mixes and frozen foods; women spend less time
in kitchen, prepare quick meals.

After business session, dance held for members and
wives. Music: Milton's Musicmakers.

Convention closes with business session this morning.
Speaker: Walter B. Johnston of Memphis, executive vice
president of a chain of supermarkets in that area. Talks
on merchandising. Says more care should be given to dis-
playing merchandise. Study the store arrangement; see
that it's easy to find various articles. Keep store lanes
open.

Association elects officers for coming year: President,
Arley C. Pierson of Coldwater; vice-president, Thomas D.
Butler, Jonesville; secretary-treasurer, Ralph R. Robinson,
Clarkston.

Association discusses where next year's convention will
be held. Invitations extended by members from Portland,

17

Holton and Grossboro. Vote is taken; Grossboro is
selected.

During morning bus tour for wives of members; visit
historic places, Jonesville and Adams county.

Two hundred persons (including wives) at convention.

5 / EXCHANGE CLUB CONFERENCE

You are a reporter for the Star. It is Saturday; two-
day conference opening today at Jonesville Hotel; district
conference of Exchange clubs. Officers of Exchange
clubs throughout state attending.

Registration started at 10 a.m. today. Noon, luncheon.
1:30 p.m., first general session. After recess, workshop
sessions for different officers: Presidents, vice
presidents, program chairman, and publicity chairmen.

You attend luncheon. John L. Murphy of Grossboro,
Exchange Club regional vice president, principle
speaker. Welcoming address: Russel M. Quinn, president of Jonesville Exchange Club, and Mayor Baker.
Fred E. Weissgerber of Jonesville, general chairman
of the conference, tells you that 150 Exchange members
have registered; 125 accompanied by their wives.

Murphy in talk outlines conference goal: to help officers
carry out duties and improve programs of clubs. Kramer
tells you that representatives are here from clubs in
Grossboro, Gilead, Warren, Trenton, Huntertown, Oxford,
Shelby, Byron, Hobart, Rockdale, Clinton, Morton and
other cities in state.

Workshop sessions this afternoon for different officers;
those in charge are: Presidents, Murphy; vice presidents,
Henry C. Gafford, Jonesville; program chairmen, Theron
E. Sullivan, Hobart. Gafford is a member of the national
board of control. Above men will also be in charge of
workshop sessions for officers tomorrow morning. All
sessions being held in Jonesville Hotel.

Dinner-dance tonight at 8, Crystal Room, Jonesville Hotel.
Music: Pat Greene Plus Five.

Workshop sessions for officers, 9:30 to 11, tomorrow
morning, final of conference. During these sessions,

19

movie travelogue of national parks to be shown to
wives.

Write story for today's city edition of the Star,
which is off the press at about 3 p.m.

You are a reporter for the Star. Annual State 4-H Week being held at Dexter University; you cover it for today's Star.

This is Thursday. This morning 4-H Club style revue being held for state honors. The girls model clothes they have made. Several classifications; winner and runner-up for each classification. Also, a grand champion. The classes are formal, play clothes, skirt and blouse, and tailored outfit. County winners elegible to compete in today's state contest.

Results of today's competition: Formal dress, Patricia Burke, Calhoun County, winner; Mary Porter, Steuben County, runner-up. Play clothes, Edna Gavelli, Hamilton County, winner; Dorothy Hammond, Morgan County, runner-up. Skirt and blouse, Pauline Johnson, Marshall County, winner; runner-up, Edith Benson, Harrison County. Tailored outfit, Carol Foust, Jefferson County, winner; runner-up, Suzanne Fountain, Clay County.

Judges announce Carol Foust is grand champion. Judges: Miss Rose Martin, professor of home economics, Dexter; Miss Anna L. Winston, proprietor of Winston Dress Shop; Russell W. Quin, manager of Gafford's Department store.

Grand champion of state competition gets $100 cash award. Also trip to National 4-H Club Congress, all expenses paid, in December, to compete in national contest. National competition, champion and runner-up each to win college scholarship, college of student's choice.

You talk to Miss Foust. She's 16, dark-haired, brown eyes; junior at Ottawa High School. Daughter of Mr. and Mrs. Frank L. Foust, Route 2, Ottawa. Carol says she plans to major in home economics. Probably will attend Dexter.

State 4-H Week closes tomorrow morning. Main business:
election of state officers. Present officers: Jack
Hickman, Clinton, president; Perry Dunlap, Walton, vice-
president; Janet Henderson, Lexington, secretary-treasurer.

Sessions being held in Dixon Auditorium. About 400 4-H
delegates attending. Being housed in university dormi-
tories.

You are a reporter for the Star. This evening you attend
Exchange club dinner meeting in Jonesville hotel.

After the meal Russel M. Quin, President of the club,
presides at program. Three selections by the Central
High school choir; Glen D. Stephens, choir director.
Quin calls on Edward W. Kramer, secretary. Kramer
reports on officers' conference of Exchange clubs in
Grossboro last month. Plans were completed for annual
convention to be held in Grossboro next month.

Quin calls on Paul A. Thompson. Thompson is chairman
of awards committee of local club. He says he and his
committee have selected member of club to receive annual
community service award. Winner to be revealed tonight.
Award based on service to entire community. Mr. Thompson
syas four nominees were considered. He announces that
the member selected for award is Bruce B. MacDonald.

Mr. MacDonald is manager of Robertson Electric Co.
Scoutmaster of Boy Scout Troop number 12, president of
Grace Methodist Men's Club. Also vice president of
Dexter Alumni association. Member of City Zoning Board;
he was chairman of the commercial division of the recent
United Fund financial campaign. MacDonald is presented
a placque. Thompson presents the placque. Wives of
members are guests at dinner meeting; 150 people
attended.

8 / NEW POST OFFICE

You are a reporter for the Star; Post Office is on your beat. This morning you call on postmaster, Howard L. Eckart; he says he has a good story for you.

He says he can now make announcement of something that has been developing for several months. Jonesville is to get a new post office. It is to have 18,000 square feet of floor space. Eckert says the building is to be completed within 8 months. Cost: about $800,000, including cost of land.

Building to be completely modern, air-conditioned. Bids for construction to be taken from any interested firm. Postal officials have bought site within walking distance of center of downtown business area: 100 block of East Poplar.

Jonesville post office now has 40 employes; more to be added as volume of mail increases. Eckart says new building to be constructed with future in mind; take care of needs of city for 25 years. Present building built, 1922; not much change in it since.

Late George D. Rayborn, father of present superintendent of schools, postmaster when present post office building was built. Then only 17 employes; city only about half the population it is today.

Eckart says government will sell present building to highest bidder, after new building is occupied. Government to advertise for bids for construction of new building in about a month. Eckart says building be finished about 7 months later or 8 months from now.

Property in 100 block of E. Poplar has been owned by Ernest D. Reynolds. You talk to Reynolds. Vacant house to be torn down; starting next week.

9 / COMPANY EXPANSION

You are a reporter for the afternoon paper. Assume it
is about Feb. 15. At Chamber of Commerce, the secretary,
Joe Green, tells you he understands Jonesville Manufacturing co. has some new plans. Expansion plans,
Green thinks.

You telephone president of company, Leon A. O'Connor,
ask about the report. O'Connor says he hadn't planned
to release the story until next week, but he finally
gives you the facts. He says company does plan to expand;
says new division will be added.

O'Connor says a new building will be built to house new
division. Building will cost about $900,000. Line of
kitchen utensils to be produced. Construction of new
building will be started March 1. New division will have
200 people working in it; this in addition to 700 now
working at Jonesville Manufacturing. Building to be
finished by June 15. Brick and steel construction.

After building is built, equipment to be installed.
Equipment to cost about $600,000. O'Connor says new
division should be making kitchen utensils by Aug. 1.
Building to be on company's land in 2300 block of E.
Illinois st. Short distance east of main building. New
building to be modern design, air-conditioned. 25,000
square feet of floor space.

Start interviewing applicants for jobs in new division
June 1. Albert T. Hall to be in charge of new division.
He's a foreman now. Been with company 19 years; foreman
past 7 years. He's been promoted to assistant superintendent, effective March 1. He will assist in supervision
of construction, also installation of equipment.

Write the story for today's paper.

10 / OFFICE BUILDING

You are a reporter for the Star. It is a morning early
in May; city editor tells you to drive out to Gulf
States Utilities Co. on S. Clay and see manager about
new building. Get story for today's Star.

At Gulf States you see manager, Samuel F. Edmond, in
his office. He says the company will build a new office
building. He goes to window, points to storage building
on the northwest corner of Gulf States property. Says
it will be torn down; site of new office building.
Considerably bigger than present office building.

You ask Edmond when work will start. He says tearing
down storage building will begin next week. Excavation
for new building be started by June 15. Expect to complete building by next April. Nelson and Miller of
Jonesville are the contractors. Building to cost about
$1,200,000.

Edmond says brick, concrete, and steel construction--
fireproof. Air-conditioned throughout. Three stories
and basement. Building 50 by 110 feet. Total of about
20,000 square feet of floor space. Customer service
offices on main floor. Bookkeeping department on second
floor. Executive offices, third floor. Snack bar and
employees' lounge, basement.

Edmund says Gulf States been operating in Jonesville since
1930, when bought facilities of Pioneer Utilities Co.
Expanded service during the years. Jonesville office
was made a district office two years ago. District:
Adams, Jefferson, Webster, and Franklin Counties. At
that time first started plans for new building. Office
personnel increased two years ago from 35 to 75 people;
crowded in present building. Need more space. Present
building built in 1934; about 6,000 square feet of floor
space.

29

Edmund says possible that district be enlarged in a few
years--more counties included. Company has been relocating
and consolidating district offices for several years.
He says possible for expansion of new building if necessary.
Wing could be added at one end to form L-shaped building.

You ask him what about present office building? Edmund
says it will be remodeled; used as warehouse after new
building is completed.

11 / SUBURBAN OFFICES

It's a Wednesday afternoon in July. You are a Sun
reporter. William D. Lee, secretary-treasurer of
Jonesville Real Estate co., phones, asks you to come
to his office for news story for tomorrow morning's
paper.

When you arrive, Mr. Lee goes to Jonesville city map
on the wall and points to a spot and says, "There's
where we'll do some building." He says it's the 3200
block of North Clay street. Corner of Clay and Pearson
street. You ask what the company plans to build; Mr.
Lee says, a suburban office building.

You ask Mr. Lee when they started planning that. He
says company been studying such a project for a year.
Decided definitely several months ago. Morton construction co. of Warren submitted low bid for the
building job. Was awarded contract. Four-story
building will have about 20 offices. Clearing of site
will start next week. Actual construction to start in
about 3 weeks. Lot has a 200 foot frontage on Clay,
260 on Pearson. Cost of building estimated at $1,100,000.

Parking facilities for about 200 cars, Lee says. Expect
to finish building by May 1 of next year. You ask Lee
who will have offices in building. Lee says several
tentative reservations made; expects branch bank and
insurance company on main floor; commercial firm offices
on upper floors. Also expects several professional offices--
doctors and dentists.

You ask Lee why build there. He says there's a need in
Jonesville for more office space. Parking facilities
downtown are crowded. Some offices don't need to be
downtown, but parking is important. So such a location
is ideal.

31

You ask Lee what's there now. He says a vacant building
that used to be a neighborhood grocery, Porter's Market,
closed six months ago; also 3 old houses. Work of
tearing down the four buildings will begin next week.
Lee says new building will be called Spartan building.
It will be fireproof; of brick, concrete and steel,
air-conditioned.

12 / STADIUM ENLARGEMENT

You cover March Board of Education meeting tonight for
tomorrow's Sun. Thomas C. Decker, president of board,
presides. Various actions taken. You decide to make
separate story of this:

Paul T. Sanford, principal of Central high school, attends
and asks to speak. He says something should be done about
football situation, not enough seating capacity.

Present seating capacity of stadium is 5,500. Sanford
says last fall records were kept of persons standing at
the five home games. Stands filled for every game;
average of 1,100 standees. For one game, 1,800 standees.
He says the stadium should be enlarged to handle at
least 1,500 more people, maybe 2,000 to take care of
future growth.

Decker says Central Parent-Teacher association recently
adopted resolution, urging stadium be enlarged. Says
they sent him copy of resolution last week.

Sanford says he has about 30 letters from fans asking
why they don't increase seating capacity. Decker asks
Sanford if he knows cost. Sanford says informal estimates
have been made; around $15,000 to enlarge it to 7,000,
and about $18,000 to enlarge it to 7,500.

Board discusses matter; votes to increase size of stadium,
depending upon engineers' estimate for adding 1,500 and
for adding 2,000. Decker appoints comittee of board members,
Thomas G. Butler, Dr. Joseph M. Gardner, and Ralph E. Cook;
to study problem, get estimates on 1,500 and 2,000 increase,
and report at April meeting. Work will start in June, so
that stadium will be ready for first home game September 20.

33

13 / SHOPPING CENTER

You are a reporter for the Star. It's February. Shortly after you report for work this morning, city editor tells you to go to Jonesville Real Estate Co. and talk to William E. Lee, secretary-treasurer for story about shopping center.

Lee tells you that he is ready to make an announcement about shopping center to be constructed in northern part of city. Work to start first of next month. Actually, more than a shopping center; also a professional center. Location is intersection of North Lafayette and Grant. Real estate company to be owner of shopping and professional center. Company bought the property several months ago from Stanley B. Harker of Oxford. Occupied by used car lot until about year ago.

Cite contains eight acres. To be 14-store shopping center, air-conditioned, fireproof. Units connected by 12-foot canopy. They're to be constructed of steel and concrete. At right angles with row of store buildings will be professional center. Offices for four physicians and two dentists. Also steel and concrete, air-conditioned, fireproof.

In shopping center, A&P to have store; Colton Department Store to have branch; Jonesville Pharmacy to have branch. Other stores to include shoe store, dime store, restaurant, laundry, barbershop, men's clothing store. Stores to total about 70,000 feet of floor space. Paved parking area for about 500 autos.

Two offices of professional center already leased. Dr. Authur F. Young, dentist, to move from 214½ S. Lafayette; Dr. Edward D. Nelson, physician, to move from 302 Merchants Bank Building.

Shopping and professional center to cost about $2,000,000. Nelson and Miller to be contractors. Paul E. Pearson, Warren, the architect. Clearing of land to begin March 1. Construction of buildings to begin about March 20.

35

Shopping center to be ready for stores to move in by
October 1, for Christmas season. Professional center
to be ready at same time.

You are schools reporter for the Sun. You cover the
Board of Education's March meeting tonight for tomorrow's
paper. Thomas C. Decker, president of board, presides.
Various actions are taken. You decide to make separate
story of this action. In this story you make no reference
to other actions taken by board.

Robert N. Rayborn, superintendent of schools, tells board
all of grade schools in city are overcrowded. All class-
rooms have at least recommended capacity of pupils. In
about a dozen, temporary seats have been installed. Rayborn
says something should be done because number of pupils
is increasing each year. He says various sections of
city are growing, more schools should be built.

Mr. Rayborn says that worst situations are at Bradford
school in west part of city and Lampton School in south-
west. Bradford has thirty percent more pupils than
recommended capacity; Lampton 27 per cent more. Rayborn
says survey made recently. On the basis of it, estimated
enrollment of grade schools in city will increase twenty
percent within next five years, so new schools will be
needed.

Board discusses matter. They agree two new schools should
be built as soon as possible. Mr. Becker appoints committee
of three board members, Ralph E. Cook, Dr. Joseph M.
Gardner, Phillip E. O'Brien, to study problem with Mr.
Rayborn. He tells them to report to board next month
and recomend where to build the two schools, approximate
cost and size of buildings.

Board decides to submit a bond issue to people to pay
for construction at election in June, so construction
could be started this summer; that is, if bond issue is
passed by people. The schools would be ready by
September of next year.

37

15 / BOY SCOUT MEETING

It is January; Adams County Council, Boy Scouts of
America, has banquet meeting tonight in Jonesville
Hotel. You are Sun reporter covering meeting for
tomorrow's paper.

Roast beef dinner served. Music, Central High school
choir; Glenn D. Stephens is director. 300 people present.
Philip S. Kane, president of council, presides. Silver
Beaver awards given to five scouts; Robert Baker,
Fred Perry, and Harold Howerton, all of Jonesville,
Thomas O'Neill of Shelby, and Gordon Mason of Madison.
Awards presented by Robert C. Lacy.

Kane gives talk; tells what happened during past year.
"You workers are to be congratulated for the success of
the Adams County Council," Kane says. "We've had a
record year in membership and activities."

Among other things, he points out following:

Boy Scout membership increased 8 per cent. This made
a record membership of 3,220. This is 239 more boys
than previous year.

The council had special $335,000 financial campaign
during the past year. Fund drive financed remodeling
of scout headquarters; this remodeling was completed last
month. Also drive financed purchase of Camp Avondale
on Black River, north of Salem. Camp has 8 cabins;
4 more will be built, starting March 1. Camp will be
ready for use this coming summer.

During year 992 advancements were earned by scouts. Of
this total 640 went to Cub Scouts, 324 to Boy Scouts,
and 28 to Explorer Scouts. Also, Boy Scouts were awarded
780 merit badges. Kain says complete safety program
being mapped out for Camp Avondale. Was operated as
private camp for about 10 years before being sold to

scout council. Kane predicts a successful year for
council this year. With remodeled headquarters and
new camp, expects new membership and activity records
in the future.

You are a reporter for the Star; schools are on your beat. It is late in June and you have been told there is to be state PTA meeting in Jonesville in July. You have been told Dr. Phillip F. McDonald of Dexter U. is member of committee pertaining to meeting, so you look him up when you go to Dexter this morning.

McDonald tells you meeting is annual three-day leadership conference. Sponsored by State Parent-Teachers association and Dexter University. To be held on Dexter campus. Most sessions in Agricultural Hall. Dinner and one general session in Harris Hall. McDonald is member of steering committee which is arranging conference. Mrs. Leon W. Porter, Jonesville, is chairman. Other members: Mrs. Peter F. Galviano, Jonesville; Mrs. J. W. Brewer, Grossboro; Mrs. John T. Callahan, Huntertown.

Conference will be July 25,26 and 27. Theme is "Today's Child--Our Greatest Challenge." Registration to start at 1 p.m., July 25. First session, 2:30. Mrs. Howard A. Hall, Jonesville, president of state PTA, to preside at this and succeeding sessions. Welcome to visitors: Dr. James A. Gardner, president of Dexter.

General sessions, July 25, 2:30 p.m.; July 26, 8 p.m.; July 27, 9 a.m. Group sessions, July 26, 9 a.m. and 1:30 p.m. Group sessions for unit presidents, council presidents, district directors, and program chairmen.

Principle speaker for conference: Mrs. Leon Costen of Denver, regional vice president of the National Parent-Teachers Association. To speak at opening general session on aims of national organization. Take part in group sessions for unit presidents. To give evaluation of conference at final general session.

Evening session, July 26, panel on proposed legislation affecting schools; talk by State Sen. Frank E. Wilson,

Rockdale; also that session, talk by Mrs. Paul T. Schmidt, Grossboro, state PTA vice president.

General session, July 27, talks by Dr. Howard A. Jackson, dean, College of Arts and Sciences, Dexter, and Robert N. Rayborne, superintendent of schools, Jonesville.

To take part in group sessions: For council presidents, Mrs. Schmidt; for district directors, Mrs. Arnold D. Baldwin, Oxford, former state PTA president; for program chairmen, Mrs. Callahan. Dinner to be held in Harris Hall, 6 p.m. July 26. Dr. Fred G. Tolar, professor of sociology, Dexter, to be speaker. General session at 8 p.m. also to be held in Harris Hall. About 250 expected at conference.

You are a reporter for the Sun; it's March. Dexter
University is on your beat and you are making the rounds.
You see announcement on a bulletin board that interests
you. It is about special educational trip to be taken
this summer. Two professors, Dr. Clinton R. Green and
Dr. Wesley E. Evans, are in charge. To be three-week
trip, combine education with pleasure.

You go to Dr. Evans' office to get information about the
project. Dr. Evans phones Dr. Green to come to office,
so you interview the two about trip. Dr. Evans is an
associate prof. in history department. Dr. Green teaches
geography. Trip will cover about 5,000 miles; will go
through West. Students will get total of six semester
hours of credit. Dr. Evans will teach 3-hour course
in history of West. Dr. Green will teach course of
geography of West.

Trip to be taken in a chartered bus; air-conditioned.
Most of lectures will be on bus, through public address
system. Applications being taken now for trip. 36
students to be selected. Mrs. Evans and Mrs. Green
going along as chaperones. Trip to start July 10 and end
July 30. Deadline for applications, June 15. Itinerary
to include Yellowstone National Park, Painted Desert,
Glacier International Peace Park, Hoover Dam, Lake Tahoe,
Grand Canyon, and Carlsbad Caverns.

First time Dexter has tried this type of summer course
work. Other colleges have been doing it for several
years with success. Dexter trip, students can earn
undergraduate or graduate credit. If for graduate
credit, additional term paper required, to be written
after trip.

Accomodations have been arranged, motels and hotels. If
trip is successful, Dexter may conduct similar trip every
summer.

43

Assume that it's a Friday afternoon in October. Annual
Homecoming being observed today and tomorrow at Dexter
University. All events have been announced in previous
stories during past several weeks. You're assigned to
cover events of this afternoon and evening and write story
for tomorrow's (Saturday's) Sun. You are also to include
events to be held tomorrow.

You go out to campus where pep rally is held at Harmon
Stadium at 3:30 p.m. Thomas E. Denton of Warren, president of Student Senate, presides. Presents members of
football squad. Several student leaders give pep talks.
Music, Dexter university Band. Crowd estimated at 700.

This evening you return to campus and attend the Home-
coming Dance, Morton Gymnasium. Orchestra for dancing,
Overton's Off-Beats of Grossboro. Intermission, Home-
coming Queen candidates are presented: Mary Ann Brannon,
Jonesville; Dorothy Jordan, Jonesville; Patricia Edmond,
Jonesville; Phyllis Kramer, Shelby; Jean Fredericks,
Shelby. They had been nominated by student organizations.
First year that all have been from Adams County.

Students voted on 5 candidates Thursday. Results of
balloting secret until announced tonight: Phyllis
Kramer elected queen. Other four to be her court of
honor. Dr. James H. Gardiner, president of Dexter
University crowns queen. Queen and court to ride at
head of parade tomorrow (Saturday) morning. About 500
at dance.

You return to Sun office to write your story. You consult
Homecoming program and clippings and find parade to start
from campus at 9 a.m. Saturday, go east on Indiana street
to Lafayette, south on Lafayette to Illinois, west on
Illinois to Jefferson, north on Jefferson to Indiana,
west on Indiana back to campus. Ten floats entered by
student organizations. Bands: Dexter University, Central
High School, Madison High School, and Erie High School.

45

Other events scheduled. Open house, College of Arts &
sciences, College of Engineering, College of Agriculture,
10:30 to 12. Alumni buffet lunch, 12:15 p.m., Morton
Gymnasium. Football game, Dexter and Grossboro college,
2 p.m.; float winners to be announced during half-time
ceremonies.

Write your story for Saturday morning Sun, including
report of Friday events that have taken place and those
to follow on Saturday.

19 / SECURITY APPOINTMENT

You are schools reporter for the Sun. It's a Tuesday
afternoon in June; you are covering your beat. You contact Robert N. Rayborn, supt. of schools, in his office.
He has several news stories for you, including this one.

He says several years he and Board of Education have been
concerned about vandalism, thefts and break-ins at various
school buildings. Says during past year there have been
73 break-ins in city schools. Items taken included type-
writers, television sets, phonographs, movie projecters,
office machines, money from vending machines, books. Also
vandalism. Vandalism included broken windows, walls
smeared with paint and ink, library books torn up. Rayborn
says items stolen and amount to repair damage from vandalism, total estimated last school year at $18,500.

So several months ago Rayborn suggested to board, should
hire one man full-time as security co-ordinator, try to
keep thefts and damage to minimum. Rayborn says he got
idea from Los Angeles school system, which has its own
security force of several men working in co-operation with
police. Rayborn says security force too expensive for
Jonesville, but thinks one full-time security co-ordinator
would help. Says board studied matter, then recently
authorized him to hire Alfred T. Kelley, 421 S. Lincoln
Ave. He will start on job July 1. Rayborn says he can
announce appointment today. For 5 years Kelley has been
plant guard at Jonesville Manufacturing co.

Rayborn says Kelley will contact neighbors living near
various schools and ask them to call him if they see any
suspicious activities around school. Kelley will cooperate with city police. He'll keep records on janitors
who negligently leave school doors unlocked. Rayborne
says Kelley will work about 40 hours a week, but will be
on call at other times. He will check on schools, but
will patrol them on varied schedule. Won't go to same
school at same hours, so thief won't know when he may

47

show up at any school. Rayborn says Kelley's pay will be $9,000 a year, plus 8 cents a mile expense for his car.

From Rayborne's records and through phone conversation with Kelley, you learn this additional information about Kelley: Age, 38. Graduated from Central High School 20 years ago this month. Worked for Gulf States Utilities co., then became a patrolman with City Police Department 11 years ago. Was patrolman 6 years, then took job as plant guard at Jonesville Manufacturing. Married, has 2 sons and daughter, all living at 421 S. Lincoln ave.

You are a reporter for the Star. It is Monday, early in
October, first day of Fire Prevention Week. You are to
write story for today's paper on opening of program. You
are to report what happened today and also announce events
to be held later in week. All sponsored by Chamber of
Commerce; city and school officials cooperating in city-
wide observance. Events held today and report of those
to follow are all be included in one story.

This morning you go to Central High School. Mayor Alvin
Baker pulls alarm for unrehearsed fire drill. Pupils and
teachers evacuate building; takes them about three
minutes.

Then brief program in school yeard. Fire Chief William
M. Kennedy gives brief talk. Gives tips on preventing
fires. Kennedy presents $50 Savings Bond to Frank A.
Townsend, Central HS junior. Frank is son of Mr. and Mrs.
Alton R. Townsend. Frank won Fire Prevention Week slogan
contest. (His winning of contest was announced in news
story last week. This is the presentation of the award.)
His slogan: "Leave Camp With Fire Out--Not Out of Control."
Kennedy is chairman of Chamber of Commerce committee on
Fire Prevention Week.

You have clippings of previous stories on Fire Prevention
Week. Kennedy verifies or modifies events planned for
rest of the week as follows:

Wednesday, 12:30 p.m. Parade, fire-fighting equipment of
Fire Dept. Central High school band leading parade. Parade
to form on S. Marshall in front of Fire Station. Parade
route: Proceed south on S. Marshall to Indiana st., then
east on Indiana to Lafayette st., north on Lafayette to
Tennessee St., west on Tennessee to Marshall, then
south on Marshall back to Fire Station.

Thursday and Friday after school Boy Scouts to distribute
pamphlets to homes. Boy Scouts in uniform. Pamphlets
give advice on what to do in case of fire or other
emergency. Pamphlets provided by C of C.

Saturday morning, 10 o'clock. Central H.S. athletic field,
600 block of N. Jefferson. Fire-fighting demonstration,
members of Fire dept.

It's an afternoon in April; you're on your way to work
as a reporter for the Sun. You're driving in the 400
block of North Wilson when you notice that workmen have
started to tear down large, old rooming house. You
notice sign indicates that property is owned by Jonesville
Real Estate Co.

You check with William D. Lee, secretary-treasurer of real
estate firm to find out what is happening. He says old
building is being torn down to make way for new apartment
building to be erected on site.

Lee says it's to be four-story apartment building. Brick
and steel construction, fireproof, air-conditioned. Four
apartments on each floor, total of 16 apartments. Cost
about $400,000.

Razing of old frame Meyer rooming house to be completed
within a week. Construction of new apartment building
to start May 1. Nelson and Miller, contractors. To be
finished so tenants can move in by October 1.

Lee says old frame building has been rooming house for
about 50 years, he thinks. Says it used to be hotel
owned by Colton family. Suggests you call Harry C.
Colton and ask about it.

You phone Colton and he tells you about old building. He
says it's oldest building in town. Built by his grand-
father, Andrew J. Colton, in 1848. It was known as the
Colton Inn. For years, biggest hotel in city. Famous
guests included President James Buchanan, President
Andrew Johnson, Mark Twain and Buffalo Bill.

Andrew Colton prominent citizen in Jonesville's early
days. Was lieutenant governor of state from 1866-68.
Harry Colton's father, John C. Colton, born in old
hotel in 1860. Harry Colton also born in inn. Harry

51

Colton sold hotel in 1903.

Colton says city's big social events were held in hotel
for many years. One of most elaborate was reception for
President Buchanan in 1858.

You are a reporter for the Sun. City editor tells you
to attend meeting of congregation of First Presbyterian
church tonight to get story for tomorrow morning's paper.
He says Rev. Dickerson told him it's about a youth center.

You go to church shortly before meeting opens so that
you can talk to Rev. Dickerson. He tells you that church
has been thinking about a youth center for some time.
First considered it nearly year ago. Board of Deacons
has been working on matter; has now arrived at plan.

Meeting opens. Henry D. Boling outlines plan. He is
chairman of board of deacons. Answers questions of
members of congregation. One-story building planned;
at rear of church property on N. Jackson ave. Basement
under front half of building. Main floor would have
large lounge. Also recreation room and kitchen on main
floor. Automatic record player in lounge; dances and
other social functions could be held in lounge. Table
tennis and pool tables in recreation room. Reading
nook in recreation room. Building of frame construction.
Hobby department for boys and girls in basement. Training
in woodwork, metal work, leather craft. Metal work to
include jewelry, such as bracelets, rings, etc. Other
activities could be added later.

Youth center would be open late afternoons and evenings
and weekends. Boling says board estimated cost at $100,000.
Rev. Frank L. Kennedy, assistant pastor, would be in charge
of youth center. Kitchen fully equipped. Youth groups,
including Westminster Fellowship, could have dinner
meetings. Volunteer adult instructors and leaders from
congregation for hobby department.

Rev. Dickerson tells congregation youth center would by
good investment. Says this type of thing helps curb
juvenile delinquincy. He describes youth centers in
several other cities in state. Several members of

53

congregation take floor; say they favor plan and think it's
good thing. Glad to contribute. Several also say they'll
help with hobby department.

Congregation votes to adopt plan. Boling names committee
to conduct financial drive to finance it. Arthur N.
Harper, Chairman. Others on committee: John E. Trent,
Howard A. Hall, Joseph B. Lacey, Harvey R. Eckoff.
Harper says his committee can raise money in cash and
pledges in two months or less.

Boling says when money pledged, bids can be taken.
Construction could start about a month later. Thinks
building be completed in about 3 months. So youth center
could start operation in six months.

Harper says committee will meet next Monday night at 7:30
in church parlors. Will map plans for financial drive;
draw up teams of solicitors. Asks for volunteers; 14 hold
up their hands and say they will help solicit cash and
pledges.

You return to office. City editor says it will make good
story; wants complete story with all pertinent details
included.

You're a police reporter for the afternoon paper. It's
a Monday morning. There was a weekend burglary, and
the Sun carried the following story this morning. You
have the clipping and you check with police, but there
are no new developments. Consequently, you rewrite the
story, attempting to give it a fresh twist. You hope
to disguise story so that reader won't recognize it as
a rewrite.

Diamonds, watches and other jewelry worth more than
$20,000 were stolen when the Tucker Jewelry Co. store,
218 E. Illinois St. was broken into sometime during the
weekend.

The burglary was discovered when Norman A. Tucker,
522 Forest st., president of the firm, opened the
store this morning at about 8:30 o'clock. City police
estimated the burglary took place sometime Saturday
night or early Sunday morning.

Detectives Fred C. Huston and William R. Spencer
said their investigation showed that the burglar, or
burglars, entered the building by breaking the glass
from a rear window, reaching inside to unlatch it, and
prying off protective iron bars.

The intruders punched out the dial on the combination
of the outer door to the safe and used an acetalene
torch to burn the lock off the inner door, the detectives said.

A complete list of the missing items was not avail-
able, pending an inventory; but the stolen jewelry included
a large number of cut, unset diamonds, diamond rings,
and expensive watches. The loot included a wedding set
valued at $2,500.

Some $2,000 in cash in a small drawer inside the large,
walk-in safe was apparently unnoticed by the intruders.
Another $100 in the cash register in the main part of
the store was untouched. Several thousand dollars worth
of jewelry displayed in the store also went undisturbed,
officers said.

A tear gas bomb mechanism on the door of the safe, which was set to be triggered if the safe was forced open, was found intact near where the burglars entered the building. Detectives said the intruders used a gas mask owned by the store. The mask was found outside the rear of the building in an alley leading to Michigan St.

Once the burglars gained entrance to the building, the detectives said, they pulled the front blinds and took a mirror from the medicine cabinet of the rest room and placed it where they could spot anyone who entered the rear window. The detectives said it undoubtedly was a "professional job."

Several jewelry boxes were left scattered about the 3-by-7-foot safe.

You are a reporter for the afternoon Star. Jonesville
police have been conducting campaign to reduce traffic
accidents. City editor tells you to rewrite story
carried in Sun. He reminds you to disguise story so
reader won't recognize it as a rewrite. He tells you
to paraphrase Jackson's statement, quoting him indirectly,
rather than directly. The Sun story follows:

The lane switcher is the most frequent and dangerous
violator in Jonesville driving, police report.

The driver who constantly switches from lane to lane
on multi-lane streets is not only a hazard to himself
but his actions are a threat to all motorists around
him, police said.

Front-to-rear collisions, side-swiping and accidents
at intersections often are the result of motorists'
taking evasive action in an unexpected situation caused
by a driver who darts from lane to lane.

Directional signs such as "left turn only" must be
obeyed if safety is to be maintained. Such signs not
only reduce the chance of accidents, but also increase
the flow of traffic.

Police Chief Alvin E. Jackson gives the following
advice concerning the improper use of lanes:

"A driver must use his intelligence and plan in
advance to travel the lane best suited for moving
to his destination, changing lanes only when lawfully
passing another vehicle or preparing to make a lawful
turn.

"He should give other motorists notice of his intentions
by signaling and never make sudden movements without
warning.

"He must observe and obey all directional signs. A
good driver has his route planned so he isn't forced
to make an unwanted turn or violate lane markers.

"The key to proper lane usage is common sense and
courtesy, factors every driver must develop fully if
he is to travel safely on the increasing number of

modern, multi-lane expressways."

Jonesville recorded an all-time high in its annual
traffic fatality toll with 12 deaths recorded last year
in the city limits. There were nine the preceding year.

It is early in November. You are a reporter for Sun.
The city editor gives you a release bearing an Evanston,
Ill., dateline: Number of finalists selected in national
scholarship program. Each newspaper receiving it also
gets list of finalists in the state in which newspaper
is published. The city editor tells you to rewrite story
for Sun, using all the pertinent general information, but
naming specifically only the finalists living in the
Sun's circulation area.

The text of the general release follows:

EVANSTON, Ill.--Nine hundred eighty-five finalists have
been named in this school year's National Achievement
Scholarship Program, the National Merit Scholarship Corp.
of Evanston announced today.

They were selected from 5,500 seniors nominated by
nearly 1,600 high schools from throughout the United
States. The selection committee will study further
the qualifications of the finalists and name 200
winners of four-year scholarships.

The scholarships will range from $250 to $1,500 per
year. Continued satisfactory work on the part of the
student automatically renews the scholarship up to the
maximum of four years. Financial need is not considered
in selecting finalists and then winners, but does govern
how much financial help a winner will receive.

Winners will be announced in February. They may attend
any accredited college or university of their choice.

The list of finalists for this state, showing name, school
and city, follows:

Mary A. Briggs, Lincoln High School, Rogers; John E.
Denham, Antioch High School, Antioch; Fred R. Evans, Central
High School, Jonesville; Helen L. Gage, Broadview High
School, Marlon; Marie D. Harper, Central High School,
Lafayette; Paulette A. Kelly, Washington High School,

59

Trenton; James B. Kline, Ross High School, Rossville;
Eula D. Kramer, Jasper High School, Warren; Frank C. Lacy,
Central High School, Clifton; Brenda S. Lott, Prairie
High School, Dixon; Charles C. Lowery, McKinley High
School, Morton; Irma M. Mantle, Madison High School,
Madison; Emily J. McDonald, Capital High School,
Grossboro; William T. Parkett, Downey High School,
Downey; Donald A. Perkins, North High School, Sullivan;
Sylvia S. Price, Northside High School, Lindsay; Ruby
L. Scott, Central High School, Jonesville; Paul T.
Trent, Capital High School, Grossboro; Patricia A.
Wilson, South High School, Kingman; and Hilliard D.
Young, Porter High School, Girard.